Seren Selections

Seren Poetry

Seren Selections
edited by Amy Wack

seren

Seren is the book imprint of
Poetry Wales Press Ltd
57 Nolton Street, Bridgend, Wales, CF31 3AE
www.seren-books.com

The right of The Authors to be identified as the
Author of this Work has been asserted in accordance with
the Copyright, Designs and Patents Act, 1988.

ISBN 1-85411-404-2

A CIP record for this title is available from the British Library.

The publisher acknowledges the financial assistance
of the Welsh Books Council.

Printed in Hoefler Text by Bell & Bain, Glasgow

Cover painting: 'Deep Sun' by Prudence Walters

Contents

Tiffany Atkinson

Zoë Brigley

Abi Curtis

Karen Goodwin

Viki Holmes

Rhiannon Hooson

Huw Jones

Paul Steffan Jones

Markus Lloyd

Kathryn Simmonds

Michael Arnold Williams

TIFFANY ATKINSON

Re: Venus

Setting Year Nine to write about a place
they love, I think of your brother's dripping
doorstep, which I don't love, him neither,
but he sets your Tadcu's telescope in the road
despite the ferret, the baby, the eighth smoked
already; and it's Venus, specifically, I don't
see, which has little to say about meaning while
Morrissey busks through the outdoor speakers,
the boys roll butterfingered spliffs and hawk
love, albeit in not so many words, and I'm all
for your white shirt spooking the damndark road,
a vixen's cry (which might yet be the squeak
of a back door, somebody calling the cat home),
the spark of your lighter; the closer constellations.

The Man Whose Left Hand
Thought It Was A Chicken

did some things remarkably well, like
catching flies and finding dropped earrings
or contact lenses. Others – making omelettes
say – he learned to perform with his left hand
deep in a pocketful of seed. Mere incidentals
if your arm does chicken from the elbow down.
At times, for sure, sheer cock: up well before
he was, especially if his woman was in town,
cock-hand was known to arc at strangers in the pub
or jump soft objects. Shopping for fruit with cock-
hand was no joke. But there was hen-hand too,
heat-seeking, full of mild compulsions. This bird
knew a thing or two about the secret berries of
his lover's flesh, the dust-bowl of her back. And
rumbled the acorn growing in her breast, and fluttered
at her cheekbones till she slept. And for the kids
alone, the crazy bantam-hand of *knock-knocks*,
now-you-see-its. Still. To say the sun's play through
his fingers made the brightest comb, to say he
crossed the road more often than required, to say
he only ever drove an automatic, never got promoted
and was photographed more often than he liked, to
say he almost had his own eye out a hundred times
is not to say the man was not his own man. No. He
was a flock of tangents and surprises. And without
him we have lost all memory, all possibility of flight.

Woman Running

All runs rehearsals. For that
final loosening of breath, un-
bolting of flesh from what's
known. Tap open any runner's
knee-joints, learn the rise and fall
of her home town, how she braces
herself for desire: its reach, the bite
of its climbs. For this she lives the
also-rans of most days. Don't expect
thanks. She is running to escape you
all. Her blood's flag beats high, and
her heart's (for now at least) her own.

The Anatomy Lesson of Dr Nicolaes Tulp, 1632

Hanged for thieving a coat in the raw new year
Adriaenszoon lies on the slab for Dr Tulp,
who takes the stage in sweeping gallows black.
The good guildsmen of Amsterdam flock round
in a quackery. This Tulp has a feeling for light
and shade. Behold how he unpicks the knot
of the offender's left hand, the insinuating scalpel
paring back skin like the peplum of a tulip. Such
immaculate work: the smooth-cheeked spectators
press in, anaesthetized by high, white ruffs, purveyors
of tendon and carpal. With watchmaker's nicety,
Tulp applies forceps to the *flexorum digitorum*,
and the dead man's hand becomes fist. All is decorum
as the deadpan Doctor makes a case of Adriaenszoon.
The gentlemen, for the most part, keep their corruption
at arm's length. Tulp's in up to the neck. Between them
they'll have two coats off the poor man's back.

For a Housewarming

For our garden keeps its flint heart
under weeds. For we've crawled all morning
with iron and blade, and barrow and spade
can hang for a workday. For these are holidays.
For the neighbours play tangos in the back yard
and booze through the long arc of the afternoon.
For you drive out for wine and tobacco
and I breathe the kitchen's vapour:
hot potatoes, bruised mint, lamb roasting
slowly away from its bone. For up in the high room
there's a bed made ready like a revellers' table. For there
we'll undo ourselves against raw board and plaster.
For we all feel the heat. For thunder sounds the valley now,
jamming the radio's quiet groove. For pigeons on the eaves
take fright now; beating softly down, down.

Aberystwyth Short Fiction

And if there's a punchline, it's
police tape cordoning the lamp-post
by the deli, the police patrol all day

as folk baffled past with parcels of
pastrami, all because someone's Jack
Russell cocked its wee leg at a kink

of faulty circuitry. Wham-bam! Kentucky
fried. Unlucky. But a moral for the loose-
flied lads in the Black Lion there, who'll

never know how close they came. And if
there's a subtext, its Friday next, the small
hours outside Spar, my mate and I barely

in possession of our own names, the whole
street boxed off by the dark italics of police
and students hanging from their third-floor

windows, some kinda bust-up, same old
same old, move along now please, and what
you'd miss with all the flash and grab. Was

someone's girlfriend biting down on some-
one's name. Her face a broken glass where
maybe just that afternoon a brimming cup

had been. And further back or deeper down
beneath. The same moon standing by like
an anaesthetist. The old sea sucking its teeth.

Coffee Shop, Tuesday am.

These are the casual lines of mid-workday-morning
sunlight: teaspoons on china, kitten-heeled feet,
and the bright plastic horror of the teething-ring –
my mother's laugh, almost, on the up-beat.
Infants sprout from laps like they might spill,
worn like the sharpest fashions of the season:
their mothers thought I'd be behind the till,
or not sat here, at least, without good reason.
I've come to browse the papers, have a smoke,
but there's buggies double-parked inside the door,
so I'm reapplying lipstick for the bloke
I picked up in a bar the night before. He's
tall, unshaven, half-dressed for the fun of it,
reeking of sex, as it happens, and they're having none of it.

Sonnet to Hand-Rolled Golden Virginia

You are right. It does come first. White
touchpaper thin as a host, then gunpowder,
fuse, and the rest will follow, sure as breath.
Little promethean acts that set the world
alight. Ritual origami for the spiritually lost.
Forgive the quick intimacy at bars and parties,
for we know each other in the lung, the heart;
smoke-screen wizards all. And I a good enough
person otherwise. I take the stairs. Buy vegetables.
Am a paid-up member of Amnesty International.
I hold down a job, between fag-breaks. Angel I am
not. Everyone needs forgiving. So forgive me, but
I won't quit. And if this helps you to overlook my
other, many, far more grave shortcomings, so be it.

Nine Miles Stationary:

we stretch from our vehicles like molluscs,
raw flesh bared to a flaring sky. Fair play,
I never figured Swindon for the promised
land. A girl grits her heels on the hard shoulder,
sporting an inexplicable ballgown at high noon.
She spits into her mobile's cut-throat blade,
I fucking said I fucking *don't know*. And
my father, loving nothing like emergency,
is on the phone too – *should've checked first,
should've...* Though my life has not, once, yet,

proved urgent. Some kid on the inside lane
can't wait: his mother strips him businesslike
and points his little penis at the verge, even from here
his face a clap of rage. Meanwhile the queue grows
rearwards like a German sentence back to Bristol,
where I stopped to squeeze into my dark dress. Ellie,
take it as the crow flies, I may have to bury you
out here, though being on time would still have been
too late. Lilies, exhausted, on the passenger seat;
their scent given up on the wreath of my own heat.

Persistent Cough

This cough... they can't
account for it. No symptoms
but the weird aeolian chord
that rips open sleep like a brown-
paper envelope. No pain and it
expresses nothing, but I'm full
of the great outdoors. Blame that
indigo Sunday, a bright day cut
on the bias and spliced with wind.
I ran for miles, had spent a night
with you, was jangling with love,
had not resumed my safe Euclidian
shape. I breathed wind and it stayed
in. Elsewhere, surely, a displaced
umbilicus of air describes my inner
space *just so:* a local sensation on
the scale, say, of a whorl of petals
or a moment's funnelled breeze. And
all night through I sound my tubercular
bells. The wind more powerful than me.

ZOË BRIGLEY

from THE LESSER SECRETS: A 21 CARD TRICK
V. The Clarinet Player

The Hierophant

United by the hierophant, we bridge the sacred mysteries, bow to God's mouth.

I don't know whether to love or hate the clarinet player;
at night, notes inch through the walls from two doors down,
spin through air, patter on the windowpane. Her room is full
of clutched possessions: a wooden cupid, champagne flutes,
                                        a yellow dress
thrown on the back of a chair, silk underwear in glistening layers.

Before the concert, a bright scent in the hall;
her hair is tied up in tight, little knots so the bloom
of her cheek is free to breathe. Onstage her skin is transparent
under light; she straightens her back in the midst of the music,
her lips part and she blows life into wood.
                                        Patterns of notes for
a busy street, a mouthful of teeth, a yellow dress. Words lose pitch
when I close my eyes: music seeping in like light under a door.

X. My Grandfather*

gripped his thigh when the long line of planes took
off, his knees bunched in
the rear gunner cockpit. Light pierced the dense
thicket of noise, so
when he peered through the misted glass,
he glimpsed
a face in the plane parallel; the cast
of his friend was a
pale print lit for an instant and
then gone.

The drone of the engine continued its
constant humming and
he was rocking in time with the engine's
perpetual growl.
He thought of the dead at home when the plane
flew over a map
of lights–the German town they had been sent
to bomb–and the flash
and growl when the city was hit soon faded
in the engine's drone.

On the ground, he queued in the line of men
waiting to draw a wide, white tick next to
their names; by one name, no mark:
a black space on the board filmed with dust:
smoke over the night sky.

*The Wheel

XIX. She*

The Sun

after T.H. Parry Williams

I arrived with the last snow of spring, erred across
to burrow in mountains (too small to be a loss).

A rough patch of skin on the sole of a foot, her clutter
causes slight dismay to those who believe in order.

Trace the bones of a country buried deep in her, or
grin at litany and nation and a native's core.

Her lovers are unmentionable; the dull drone
to fill her emptiness: the whine of a trombone.

The muzzle of red light loses its bite far from herds
of dumb animals–extremists bleat empty words.

Wind rakes hair, lacerates clothes screaming over rough terrain
at the mountain top. My imagination: a steam train.

Heaviness of cloud tumbles over land,
fields raked like people's pockets. So I scan

the horizon for the house where I was born: here
native voices tucked in brickwork are just as clear;

her hair nets my imagination, her roots
wrap my bones, my skull pinned underfoot.

*A version of 'Hon' by T.H. Parry Williams

XIII. A Small Unit of Time

Death

For that which is born, death is certain...
Therefore grieve not over that which is unavoidable.
                                        The Bhagavad-Gita

Some nights he'd make a cup of hot chocolate
before we went to his room: the kitchen
that always smelt of roast beef, milk in a mug
and the microwave timer ticking down.

I stared at the digits, dismantled them with my eyes,
numbers that appeared and vanished in the flash of lines.
Milk bubbling, the mug on the table where I sat,
the jar of chocolate and heaped teaspoons.

I stirred it slowly until the milk turned brown
and the steam was coated with the powdery smell.
Trying to drink it slowly, I ran my tongue
round the mug's rim, placed it on the mantelpiece.

"Haven't you finished it yet?" He waited
lounging in front of the TV, legs sprawled open.
I read the TV guide, filled up the time with my voice;
by then it was too late and he had to drive me home.

XXI. Trade*

Now the oceans
are mapped, we sail deep
into strange continents where people
are small and dark, where most never leave
the parish of their birth. Up the hill from the port,
I rub at the window of the shop with a soaped cloth;
Señor Vasquez leans in the doorway, his soft body bulges
under his shirt. I stop for a moment to look down the hill at
the white sails of shops; the boats come in full of sugar, flax
and cotton from countries that no one has visited. I pronounce
a name, try to imagine its people: flax and linen from *the Baltic*,
oranges from *Greece, Colombian* physalis. When the window is
clean, I scrub with a broom at the pavement, at the red dust
caught in the grouting, the red dust smudged on hands and
faces, settled over clothes. He yawns in the doorway and
as I polish the black tiles on the shop front, I dream
of the marketplace: green and purple vegetables,
silver strung beads, blue bottles of elixir and
medicinal powders made by a woman
living high on a hill above boats
sailing in, the port.

*The World

Barb

The hook and curve of the window once held kites of glass red and blue, but now
they frame the grooves of brickwork in a wall, leaves blinking in a canopy
of eyes, saints wedged in corners, a glass chandelier lights a window.
The cathedral bears no roof, so when I look up there's only
thick, black sky; the last tower points up into the night.
I sit on the bench, wrap my coat tight round me.
You stand in fine rain spinning under light:
dust rising from a blast. The surface
of the stone is shiny and bright.
Blurred reflections interlace
shadows in the red glint
of street lamps. Faces
study a large cross
in split wood,
dark moss
mud.

from THE GREATER SECRETS: A 20 DAY ROUND
My Dress Hangs Here*

on a washing line over the city;
a woman's flag, threaded with lashes
of eyes, of windows, desire and pity,
measures time with its tightening seams.

It is the receiver where I listen
to breathing at the end of the line,
or the bridge I cross myself in search
of a dull silhouette in the green river.

My dress is a queue of women each jostling
the other to inch forward a small step
or it is an artefact on display
photographed in brown newspaper clippings.

Passive, maternal, childish, aspiring,
crazed, ablaze, frank, enraged,
broken, resistant, grateful, appealing,
plaid, patchwork, clue—my dress.

*Day 11: Ozomatli, the great orator, sculptor and writer of glyph from Aztec
legend, was lured into the tree by the jealous brothers and transformed into
an ape, a monkey god.

from THE CURSE OF THE LONG TAILED BIRD

Space-Time

Ordinary time appears to stand still on the horizon of a black hole.
                                                        –Stephen Hawking

Here is an island like a jewel or scarab
on the flat lagoon where the herons wade;
we walk the circle of main-street from town-hall door
to town-hall gate and find that every pathway
leads to the waterfront where birds wing air currents
like iron filings in paths of magnetism.

A buzzard of the Mexican highlands is drawn
by this feeding ground of turtle, shrimp and beetle:
gods that fell headlong from the sun's ripening course
to merge with the earthbound souls of the dead
and plague them invisibly for life and vigour,
the buzz of regret eclipsing the Milky Way.

You show me the stars of the southern hemisphere
Here, the beekeeper wooing the hives with his charms,
and here, a lady–Obsidian Butterfly
spelled with stars, throwing arrows against tidal winds.
No more of the past, that which has always happened,
a remote island that jolts to life each day.

Lying on the pier, I put an eye to the slats:
the lagoon's quiet pulse of bird foot or paddle
teaches me to hear and know a bird arced in space,
a pebble thrown up over water in the dark.
The sky will persist for a thousand years and I
will remain here young, in search of the Southern Cross.

ABI CURTIS

In-betweens

I can't help noticing,
tying my shoelaces:
those eyelets let them through.

That's how it is with you,
the soft gap of your mouth
allowing the traffic

of breaths, whispers and words.
Pin-pricks in your ears for
threading lines of silver.

The million lips of pores
are channels for your scent
into the fibres of

your clothes; in turn fastened
through their white button holes:
covering the folded

skin that joins your middle,
vanishing to the star
deep inside your belly.

All this, as you're stretching
to the shelf, sighs living
beside each strand of hair;

fingers slipping a book
into its empty slot,
toes poised on ladder-rungs.

Are the pages settling?
Eyes slide round sockets to
seek me through sifts of dust.

I rise from my lacing,
try to resist blinking
to keep what's between us.

The Cupboard

...the word-hoard is not a cupboard... – Northrop Frye

A tile of light lifts
a shift of onion skins aside.

Potatoes, nobbled with time,
rock forward as giant toes,
earless but listening

to lids click,
and a spider spangling her lines of thought:
a twist of white between
the wood and where it splits.

A crane fly, startled he's alive,
tip-toes the toolbox,
risking his fragility on nails and wires
menacing to himself.

Dropping slowly from the shelf
he leaves

a leg behind:
a pencil-mark, an underline.

The spider trawls him.
Then with herself she quickly sews him:
a thin of wings,
a mess of legs,
wrapped and over-wrapped in threads.

A duster turns a feather,
recalling flight and water,

while the spider
finishes her package
then stacks it neatly
with the others.

Mountain Li-Po

Snow-peaks balance a silhouette.
A climber pauses in awe.
Sunlight dangles at the summit.
Ropes lengthen to an eyrie.

A hare dashes from the plant-tufts,
snuffling for flowers of air.
His paws collapse the moutainside;
a life sweeps off, mid-sentence.

New Lover

A woman you have never met
is touching you through his finger-tips,
adding her soft gravity to his
tougher sinews, presence-less in your bed.
Gentled kisses applied from his lips,
a trace of her face inside his head,
but none of her concocted scent
or words like weightless gifts:

only the brew of you and him filming his skin.

Though in pressures upon your edges,
she draws you in the damp silks of body-hinges,
tracing your lines in her own image:
the memory of a night two women shared
when neither she, nor you were there.

Flirting with Poets

There are some wonderful words in English,
he says softly, like "Swish",

as he leans forward in a corner of the bar.
She sips from her glass

shows agreement with her eye-lashes.
"Lunch" is one, its sound matches

a bite into bread. She smiles.
He shifts his weight to the arm beside

her head, adds "Elbow" in a whisper.
"Mmm...Wishbone", comes her answer.

"Cushion", the word sits plumply beside them.
"Mushroom" grows out of the carpet beneath them.

"Butterfly" glitters their space in-between
"Midnight" weaves its invisible scenes.

Each one, spoken lower
makes its way over

the sharp-edged noise,
fades the swirl of voices

to the hush of a whale sleep-talking;
ancient, weightless, soothing.

Their toe-tips touch.
Her body absorbs

the silent wall
as she breathes across his lips: "Quill"

"Bliss", he sighs in reply,
so she closes her eyes

for a word that begins
with a "k" and ends

with this...

Birthday Cake

You left the house at eight to go to work,
setting down your case to kiss me first.
I think of this while I separate egg-yolk
from its white membrane,
pouring it through two halves
of its own shell.
It leaves its loose glue on my fingers.
I remember myself and my self-raising flour,
into which I've made a well.
I siphon milk in dribs and drabs,
I'm folding with a spatula
soft white gullies and sticky crags
for sultanas to populate.
A flick of nutmeg and a touch of salt
darken the floppy hills:
I think of the freckles on your neck
and the way your shirt folds twice at the elbows.
I stroke butter round the edges of a baking tin
then slow pour the mixture in.
The oven door becomes a screen
to view the rising, crumbly dome.
I wait for heat to fuse and unify
every action of today.
I wait for your return
at the turn out of your cake.
While I lick the raw ingredients from the bowl,
I wonder if it's you
or me I've made.

Cloud

Before we could travel by air
we knew them only as
the grubby underbellies of giant
white cats.

But now, above them, on the other side,
I think differently of ground:
dense, silted, packed with sediment,
the opposite of cloud

with its haberdashery of vapours,
so tactile, so sure of itself.
A piping of white confidence,
stackings without shelf.

It can't be negotiated by any
human digit,
does not belong to us but to beings
formed boneless

who share the sky with us but
are invisible to our bolshy eyes,
so weightless their weightlessness
itself escapes us.

They design their villages
to shift their driftings,
tread a strange foundation –
not on or in or under
but with the cumulus,

their disappearings,
their accumulations.

The Ghost of the Nature Reserve

They found my body here:
where dandelion clocks tick,

counting the years in airborne wishes.
There is nothing more delicate than this,

except for eye-lashes
closed forever in the nettles

or miniature fingers clamped tight in the chaff,
shreds of a stranger's skin in their beds.

I melted slowly into soil;
food for woodlice, their caresses coiling

through my hair, streaked in silver
every evening by star-shine and snails,

but left alone by moths in their flimsy dresses;
they search for light elsewhere.

Glove

I realise
I have lost a glove.

Inevitable.

They seem designed
to separate –
a question

not of 'if'
but 'how':

I pressed finger-skins
against a letter's edge,

empty glove in glove.

Slip of envelope into a slot:
a necessary loss,

but I am numb
to a thumb-tip
finding the path,

and already moving on.

While the letter sinks and rises
with a thousand corners,

a passing stranger offers,
reaching for the woollen fingers.

The letter separates,
shutters through a doorway,
opens onto recognition.

A hollow hand is signalling,
signalling
from a railing
on the corner.

Shoe

Running for the train, wearing insensible shoes,
one slips and finds its way to the gap between two solids:
the platform and the train's edge.
It lies invisible on the track beneath.
I stand on one barefoot:
a startled pigeon, seeking help.
I must wait for the train to leave without me
as I flex each naked toe in turn and grieve.

I remember my mother's story:
Her first day at school, her soft new shoes,
a round, perfect button on each,
the man that stood on her and sent one to the track,
the train than came and went
and that battered shoe that could not be replaced.

My train was ticking up its steely blood
when the litter-picker wandered up,
long-limbed, long-eyed, his head
seemed to float above his neck as if
hanging from the felted clouds
on a string of rain.
His metal gadget like a limb-extension
opened its angled fingers and lengthened
to the shadows beneath the train.

A moment passed until
the shoe came back
attached to the gravity of the grab.
It was intact.

As the train rolled out with me inside, I turned
to wave and thank my helper
for his silent hand.
But there were only pools of darkness
on the platform,
accepting whatever reflected in them.

KAREN GOODWIN

Piercing

Angling the lamp close
he pores over me like a textbook,
my stomach flattens
under his hands – a lit page.

He reads the lines,
clamps a corner of flesh in metal,
then fetches his tools,
needles, ethanol, jewel.

The lamp flinches,
its hot eye of astonishment
fast at my skin – brightening
a patch where blood

swells and pools round the garnet
and his fingers working
quickly threading and capping,
stemming the flow with a towel.

Later, I remember the Mayans
who pushed thorns and rays
through their fat tongues,
how each blood-drop was a ruby
hallowed in cupped hands.

Archaeology

Late October and mornings at the tool shed are icy,
cold metal sky bitten down on the earth,
leaving its teeth marks in the grass.

The field remembers the tracks I made to the water pump
frosting hard bracelets from my heel
preserving me in ice and mud.

The trees overhead switch and clack their blades in the wind,
hurriedly unforking their bundles,
having nothing to do with the earth's attachment

to living things, they leave no visible trace –
washing their arms to the elbows,
shedding their dog-wet scents.

I break open the grass crust, lever and slough
spadefuls of soil, remaking it
over my shoulder, bailing myself out of a mud boat

cut from my image.
I want to get to the bottom of it,
the water table, the rocks, the roots

leaching themselves white as lime
to the field's floor.
And here I find what I am digging for –

the tree's root wrapped tight round
a blunt stone, a child's hand frightened in the darkness,
grips and won't let go.

My Mother's Hands

Talk, measure a world,
a pair of wings.
I watch them shape
the emptiness –

phrase and rephrase,
sculpt the rise
and fall of speech.
My mother's hands

pick arguments,
wringing a tea-towel
of its dampness,
lighting a cigarette,

her fingers ticking on wood.
My mother's hands
change daily,
pouch and beg,

show themselves
innocent as coral,
and blind in the light
retract, hurt.

My mother's hands
fly up like stamped dust,
cartwheel,
repeat themselves

spoke after spoke.
My mother's hands
turn inward
beaten and pitted.

Fitting my hand
to hers in sleep
like a leaf
shadowing a leaf,

a thing to grow against –
her print still warm
on my thigh,
lifting off its red.

Nain's Funeral

These lilies, stars
wafting their death scent
over the grass, the plastic, my hands
where I clutch her charm bracelet
like a rosary.

Counting off spoon, leek, cartwheel,
St. Christopher, tears of perfume,
of pure oil drop from their white faces.

Here comes the mercury
drawing its poison over the lake,
its mirror, where a graceful neck
turns through symmetry
to an elephant's wrinkled face.

Now it is night,
my window blacked-in
and these stars, lilies,
wafting their death scent.

Green Line

(UN Buffer Zone between north and south Cyprus)

I'll write you a postcard
from the inside looking out,
sketch the intricacies of a split

and damaged fruit,
how the bruised flowers
of a blackberry grow up

between rusted whirls
of barbed wire. Or note
how much like a pitted almond

a house-wall looks,
when its side has been pelted
by bullets, the craters

left by burnt shot,
remind me of their flawed whiteness.
And I'll scribble in the corner

how sad it is to witness –
whilst sunlight bathes
my skin and nettles

unfurl a new
and dangerous hand
their touch quick, serrated.

The Quince Orchard

Glancing through the car window
I thought you a ghost orchard,
the sun slipping her coat

from your shoulders.
Your bark was a nude surprise,
leafless and grey as potash

one cycle away
from wood-fossil or smoke.
I imagined the dead waking

to a winter like this,
meagre and fruitless,
a pile of used sticks.

Stiffening into a dumb embrace,
a burnt forest,
haunted citadel.

Yet, as we round the corner
I catch the flash of fire
on frost, gold

in the gloomy interior –
cupped from the dark,
bulb after bulb

string the rafters,
lighting the eaves
of an abandoned house.

Tango

I am spot-lit on the dance floor,
dress sliced to my hip, bodice encrusted with gems.
The cellist saws the strings
and my heart shivers into plumage,
my feet quicken and cut the boards
into tiny dazzling pieces.

The accordion player
stretches open his deck of cards,
like a lung filling with oxygen
before he crushes them shut with a twang of chords.
I wake feeling my chest
compressed by his strong hands.

This is my night's confession –
how I danced like a fish
thrashing spiked feet from air.
And how I find myself, salt-dry, gasping for water,
surprised by long scratches on my arms,
the cluster of bruises on my wrists.

Scissors

You are cutting my hair
With those longhandled dressmaking scissors
You keep in the top drawer.

The fingercatch a stiff spray of feathers;
A cruel spur.
They dip snapping

At my silken fronds
Like a heron.
Flashing on their hinge

Grinding fishbones
To dust in my ear.
I know they are evil

Because you point them at me
Open-beaked, their long jaws
Hanging mid-air,

They close with a shriek.
Afterwards, you run your thumb along the edge,
Wipe a clean seam of blood.

Portrait of Madame M.

Your hair is lush and black,
Polished to a flash of a seam,
The hairline crack

Of a sharpened pencil.
Thrown into relief,
Your cheekbones,

The pale wood underneath,
The hard-won light
Of something savoured and expensive.

The tapers of your red-lit fingers
Poking and sparking
At the place where your heart should be.

And is it your shoulders
Or your hips that surprise me?
Broad-lapped, bovine

Tied in a sash, you remind me
Of a classical pillar, a temple column
To be dressed, worshipped at.

Over your shoulder, a blue scarf
Crumples its metals
Like a rose frowning

Into a long winter
Or a soul recounting its passage
Into the depths of a cold mirror.

VIKI HOLMES

post card no. 1: winter wonderland

the city continues much as it did before you went away. lights sparkle in the trees and it's almost picturesque, you might say. people, there are many people here and every one of them thinks differently, every one occupies their own unique space. it's cold, but not as cold as previous years, just enough to make people's eyes shine. scarves are popular this year, i notice. also fairground rides, chestnuts and painted glass. pottery has fallen off slightly, there are trends even among artisans, although ethnic statues continue to do well. there is much talk of going skating on the outdoor rink. few follow up on this, although it always seems busy. i walk past on my way home most nights. just knowing it's there is enough. my way back takes me past a place that no longer exists. there used to be a kebab shop called ali baba and the forty tasty dishes. the sign was pink, with a parade of veiled, doe-eyed women. it's gone now, and i don't eat kebabs anyway, but i miss the sign. funny thing is, i can't remember where it used to be, i can't tell what has replaced it. i look at all the shop fronts, all the chippies and dry cleaners and internet cafes and i don't know which of them used to be the one i miss now. it's hardly a tragedy of unknown soldier proportions. nevertheless, i'd like to know.

do you see how this is not about love? life goes on without you and it is surprisingly compelling. nevertheless, my writing is prosaic, something is missing. i don't know what, but i imagine you might. you usually do. please send answers.

swimming lesson february 1981

the pool's edge
pocked leaves skim our milky skins:
the spit-kiss of a fractious mother
hankying a dirt-spot clean

we hinge at the belly
flip to submerge
from the rain-crash
at the water's top

follow
in the splash-foots
of those ahead
as their arms part

then meet
eyes flicker
in underwater REM,
the logic of dreams –

to keep the rain off
you must go under.

men sitting by the fountain

miss, you speak english?
>*a little, i don't know why i say a little.*

miss, you christian?
>*no, buddhist. this conversation*
>*is the wrong way around.*

miss, you hold my hand
because my head –
sorry. come sit over there
because the men
i don't want them look at me.
thankyou. miss, you hold me there
my back – because my head – sorry.
>*but he is gone.*
>*he wants to cry. he is sad,*
>*because his head –*

tighter. my hand.
thankyou.
>*by the fountain that does not work.*

miss – sorry.
>*and he is back.*

miss, you hold me
there, my back,
because
my head – miss!
>*the red sun on top of fountain*
>*and i am the only redhead here,*
>*the only girl –*

– miss!
you hold my hand. finish.
i have finish the water
by the fountain. the men
not look at me, miss.
>*this fountain works, should i*
>*be waiting by the fountain*
>*that does not work? you'll find me*
>*i'm sure, i am the only redhead here.*

here – my hand. hold tighter.
i am sad and i do not want
the men to look at me.
sorry.
miss.

how to play a drum

you will need to be aware of gaps –
how they appear and disappear –
sound is caused by contact then no contact.
the memory of how long the gap was, then its repetition.
that is rhythm: how things are the same but different.
a heartbeat, a stroke, how blood pounds at the temples,
a history. being aware of the vibrations inside and out.
you might want to lean back and close your eyes,
the better to feel, or, remember feeling.
the repetition frees you
from the worry of how this works,
allows space for the melody. do not be hesitant –
you must trust your movement. true lightness
comes from confidence, knowing when,
how much to hold back. consciousness
of the self without self-consciousness.
you will find it harder to distinguish
between yourself and the drum: where
one ends, another begins. things
will start to appear clear again,
the space of a heartbeat
no longer separates memory from experience,
you are looking back at you here now.
close and open.
breathe and pause.
while playing you may remember other rhythms.
sometimes they will distract you
from what you are playing now.
other times they will reinforce,
make new rhythms,
more complex, subtle.
recall lives, moves on.
there is not one rhythm but many, accepting this is key.
you may find it hard to imagine a time
when you were not playing the drum,
it may feel as much a part of you

as the hand that strikes its surface. more perhaps.
ask yourself, how do your fingertips feel to the drum?
at this stage you may be tempted by mirrors,
the need to watch:
losing yourself can be scary,
you may need to remind yourself
of who you are without the drum.
sometimes remembering will come as a shock,
seeing yourself and the drum
as an observer might – two separate things:
and then there is the sound of the drum, in the air,
the same air you inhale, exhale – almost
you breathe the music in. there are no boundaries,
like memory and experience they inhabit the same space:
when it is over, it is never over. the rhythm continues,
the memory of rhythm. the drum is inside you.

usquebaugh

this spirit
kaleidoscopes
my tongue
and i can hear you better
in the dark, somehow
tuned like a radio, the frequency
persists, maintains
something to hold on to
more even, than
the grip of your thighs
the sheen of a cover
thrown aside as
what little light there is
pools like sweat
at the base
of a spine, the foot
of the bed
and we are synchronous
now, the balance
of a leapfrogged hold,
while everything
around us shifts we
slip into ourselves

"from the broadly generated curve that grows proportionately ever smaller, reducing itself to nothing came the genesis of understanding for the concept of math or numbers. from everything to nothing and back again, symbolizing life and death, infinity to zero: amun represents the unknowable, and therefore the most holy."

ammonite pick it up pick it up cross your palm with 40 million years shouldn't it glow or something shouldn't the passing years show but it's just a stone sits in your hand like a toad, not moving, cold this is magic you can buy not a golden ball caught by a pool but a snail in a swamp a snail changed to stone put it on your mantelpiece put it in a box leave it waiting for a kiss to wake it petrified mollusc left rotting in a bog somewhere is it any wonder it was scared or is it flux we're worshipping a live thing turned to stone like some cool-hearted princess didn't want her prince perched on her pillow like a frog and so she kissed him quiet as a stagnant pool he slept and then she loved him (limpid as lilypads he lay) it's what we all want the blessing not decay but transformation that's the miracle we want no pain no gut and gizzard left exposed no meat no red raw flesh just bones dem bones dem dry bones our names shall live forever no pain no pain all that's left is beauty held in the hand like something Escher drew forgetting everything you ever knew forget that all you'd been was a creeping thing stuck in the mud not ever understanding what you'd seen as the years spiral on like the workings of a shell it's delicate as clockwork, watch and stop if you raise it to your ear you can hear time ticking round and round and round the bend.   **the end.**

duty free

already
you are gone
and i am noticing
girl scouts, throngs
of them around me:
other people, the rest
of the world, getting on
your plane and travelling
back home and for this
brief time far closer
to you than i and like the
movement of a hinged
door in the breeze we
move further still apart
till the joins we traced
with fingerstubs and
laced breaths stretch
through telephone lines
and words zapped halfway round the globe – instantaneous and erroneous with all
the restraint neither of us can muster – so i shoulder my bag and move around wait-
ing for my flight tasting how the air is different how the sounds are
different it's that airport trance transit feeling where it's ok to smoke standing
up and the blood rush to your temples reminds you you're still alive your body's
your own not rented out so you can lift your head up high and the blood
spins too fast and your head can't quite catch up i see you in
neon-   back-of-the-eyelids   fluency
your head in my lap,
hair laced thru' my
fingers as i watch the
light the lights the
lights and we take
off think of that
remember that
and the last thing
either of us see is the
girl white as an etching
blood at her mouth, her head
twitching as the *petit mal* takes hold and
she shakes like autumn leaves but at least she gets
to stay to stay to stay...

thai silk

so these days when i am wearing silk and my
friend says to me, it's so beautiful, can i touch
it, is this thai silk, did you bring it back with
you and i say no, i bought it here before i
went to thailand, before i even knew what
thailand was, i just saw it in the shop and it
was green like a beetle so i thought maybe i
should have it and she lays her hand on my
thigh to feel how it is smooth to the touch this
jewel-like cloth and as her palm rests, a light
pressure, i think of how your hand maybe
rested there for a while and i think of walking
through the sea so that the sand silted my
ankles and how on returning to our bed i
dropped this glowing fabric to the floor,
exchanged without pause for the weave of
your skin on mine and i think of how
everything is connected these days so that
even an innocent touch is like that of a
woman passing a stall stacked with rolls and
rolls of silk and reaching to touch to trail her
fingers lazily across as though to choose, that
easy languid movement like raking through a
lover's hair before lifting the chin to brush the
lips, that same delicate sensuality, so that for
this brief moment i am in love with my friend
whose palm rests easily on my thigh because
her touch echoes yours and because i am
wearing beetle-back green that clings to me
like water and shifts under her touch and
because I am remembering the weight of you
above me and the night hushed around us
and the light pooling the floor and she says it's
so beautiful, is that what you brought back
with you and i nod because i am like a beetle
moving towards firelight and i can't speak at
all any more.

watch the wall, my darling

the house is slow to wake, we miss mornings now they do not come, i must make a note not to get dressed in the dark: three times this week i have surprised the office by my combinations.i touch-type like orpheus, however much i know it will result in heartache *i have to look*. i wonder how you bear it? your whole face is a smile, blazing like gorse-plagued cliffs in the sunset of a careless cigarette. those cornish summers i didn't know you, for years i'd scan the horizon for smugglers, or lights, or something. maybe a chariot would descend from the sky, i don't know. waiting for the world to happen. we climbed the ace of spades and stood at the top of everything but it didn't matter. it was all beercans for magpies those days.we know better now. horizons bend, you won't fall off if you sail too far, if you climb too high god won't brush your forehead with his fingertips. but a fire blazes somewhere: lights for the wary on a dark night. if you trust it, it'll take you anywhere you like.

RHIANNON HOOSON

Crugybyddar

My grandmother picking vetch
for the back bedroom, the valley heavy
with the smell of ramsons, a pale
carpet of stars in the wood.

Waiting for mushrooms in the field
by the river, as the eggs boil for supper
and the buzzards hang from streaks
of shelved cloud above the church.

Stamping down molehills in the lawn,
the martins gathering, swooping for midges,
and I am in my red boots like the poppies
by the door, swinging on the gate.

Tracking

I smelt it, once, my mother's scent –
not the scent of her enveloping self
which meant, to me, a lit stove
and cheese to crumble into stew –

but the scent of her own childhood
announcing itself silently one summer,
as the dust rose from the track:
some bright-remembered place

where sun-dark skin flickered its own shadow
through the lush stalks of sugar cane;
where the fan sliced through tepid air
above the veranda, and she,

avoiding the sour vermouth and olive smell
of her own mother, crouched on her haunches
in the shaded dust behind the garage,
where the pistachio lushness of the car gleamed,

and Hazel's mahogany hands
wrung the thin neck of a chicken
or added beans to the can of stew
which hung above the fire.

Samhain

My mother would not have it in the house:
the urn dug from the barrow on Cefn Mawr.
Wrapped in my father's mud-cracked corduroys,

it came home strapped in the passenger seat,
fresh from the dig. My father left it in the barn,
where the owls exhale winter in their sleep.

In the house, my mother scraped frost
from the windows, put out the fire with cold tea
only to light again. Here the second season starts:

every year the same – the fizz of green kindling,
the line of books in the porch, an extra place
at the table; knife, fork, glass, plate, all put away clean.

My father leant against the rayburn, watching the barn.
Sage and broom burnt with bursts of leaf-bright flame,
crackling like oil forgotten on the stove. The sun,

slung low and heavy in the sky like blood-filled blister,
fell quickly behind the hill. I thought of the ashes
in the pregnant curve of the urn, wondered if,

in its sealed-off world, there shone a tiny sun,
trickling white light onto the landscape of ash
that slept, mindless, in its glare.

Wintering

At the first frost, when cold makes sugar
bloom meagre into the sloes, the cows
steamed the valley, down from the hillsides.

Geese woke us in the night. The larches turned
like old men toward the wind and let go.
In the house, the pipes burst, the clock
stopped ticking, water came down the chimney.

The elm at the turn in the track dropped
its last leaves, held black branches
up to the stars. In the kitchen,
my mother baked saffron into the bread –
round suns, wintering on the table.

Storm Gazing at Orrest Head

The clouds slip
their sheen
across the fells,

caught like wax
poured into water.
The heather-bruised hills;

the sun sinking slowly
into the open mouth
of the lake. It sets

the boats glowing.
Imagine their sound
as the wind rises –

clinking together
like ice in a glass.
The long grass

knots into funnels
of green, lichen
on the rocks loses

colour like breath.
My hair tears
loose,

flaps its banner
to the sky
like a russet crow.

The Sin Eater

After my great-grandfather's death,
his wife brought in a sin eater. I like
to think it had been raining, that day,
that he was weighted down with water
as she watched his approach
from her heavy-curtained window.

He must have walked up from the town,
a good half-hour's journey. His step
was light on the path, inaudible
in the steady drive of the rain.
She would have made him wait on the step,
his Sunday-suit stiff with moisture,

and his hair slipping down his forehead.
She had not bothered to stop the clocks,
and in the dark hall they ticked to her time, now.
His coat stained the floor beneath the hat stand,
and she pretended not to see, ushered him
to a straight-backed chair brought in from the kitchen.

She cooked the meal herself, served on the
second best china. The casket beneath the plate
had an enviable shine, and I imagine him
eating until the plate was clean, in small,
deliberate mouthfuls balanced on his heavy fork.
I wonder what she cooked him,

whether he liked it. I am told he was a thin man,
like a bird, as if food eaten over a corpse
could never nourish him. Besides, she would not
have given him anything rich, nothing so juicy
as a steak, nothing meaty. My great-grandfather
would not have warranted it.

Y Bedd

In a rugged steep place,
where the waves beat
against the shore at Caer Cenodir
and the gulls dive sleek

into the sullen sea, I waited.
But the weight of these stones
guards little, save names;
these names, this bone

of land where we, unflinching,
crouch to cast our lot
and bow to strangers.
On the plain; beneath the sod

of Llan Morvael; on Long Mountain
and Pennant Twrch, our space
of silence and rock; at the fords
and at the waters' meeting places

we are buried. We are silent
beneath the stones; graves,
though many, are all we have;
graves, and the ninth wave

that never comes to shore.
Turn your back on that sallow sun;
your prodigal muse
has always spoken in tongues.

The *Englynion y Bedd* – the stanzas of the graves – from
the *Black Book of Carmarthen*, record the resting places
of fallen Welsh warriors in over seventy verses.

Elan

There was a day, well into winter,
when the reservoir froze
and we threw rocks onto the ice,

and never went back to watch them sink
as the hills shrugged into their thaw.
We never thought where they

would come to rest, till now; never wondered
whose land their shapes would mark.
But now I think of the flooded valleys,

the silent villages, the quiet churches;
all those houses filled with water
and the rot of wood. I wonder how many

men are buried beneath the dams.
What do I know of war but this:
the slow rise of water; the fat silence
of a quenched thirst.

Waiting for Ganymede

I had wanted to wait for Ganymede;
wanted – suddenly, inexplicably – to watch
as it crept around Jupiter's flushed cheek.
The metal angle of the telescope

gleams sleek against the sky.
I bend to peer into that other world,
where we have found and coveted moons
like errant motes of rock caught motionless

and silent. Midnight settles over the snow,
and we, each in the crook of the other's shadow,
wait, our hands curled like dim flowers
around porcelain and milk; breathing

like bulls into the cold air. Under mine
your lips open, hot lotus blooming
into blackness. And the world we found
in the lens is forgotten.

We are washed up
on the moon's tide,
the greying dark;
waiting for Ganymede.

Bulls

Zeus has a propensity for slipping
his flesh into the shape of a bull; stretching
his tough hide over its hulking frame.

He's always at it: witness the whip
of Europa's hair as she rides him
over the receding waves, sitting daintily

side-saddle on his broad back
and wiping wind-tears from her red cheeks.
He did these things under the moon

of precedent, though – had Pasiphae not fallen
for the bull that grazed at Gortyn, Zeus
might have stuck with an eagle.

Even the women are at it: Io trod a hundred
islands as a heifer before Zeus flicked his wrist
and she grew breasts again. Best not to ask

the fate of Ariadne, nor that of poor Asterius,
her brother. And now I come to think of it
didn't I, as a child, first come to know

of men while watching the white bull
in the field behind the house? The snow
was still patchy on the ground and he,

wreathed in his own steam, had the look
of a god, even then.

HUW JONES

Progress

It's how we are, against the clock,
which hammers into early evening, jammed with
time, and all the time it's really, truly

happening, this carry-on. A patch of sunlight creeps
across a valley bottom; no-one sees it.
Someone laughs. A dart
thuds into double top; you look away. It is enough.
Such singular perfection in the maths of it,
the twist, flight, cock. That you should see it!
You who stood last night, enormous,
undefied; head back beneath the stars.
Who dared to shut your eyes.

Transmission

The way an apple's colour bleeds
beneath the skin, its wet kiss halved;
sweat and hollow weight
arched to the palm;
     all flexed,
foot crooked to chair leg,
pen poised seismograph.

Summer

Your dense flesh sweats
a message in your
sleep. I cannot find

you there: your dreams
are crowded, unfamiliar.
We meet in some old

pub, you know, just
down the road; (where
I am sort-of-known,

folded paper, half-full
glass.) The eye is
a knife, and you

no surgeon;

more a toast and butter
man – you spread
a melting word
across the room.

How Can You Know?

A smooth palm of
metal, slightly creased. We cross
the wires, a silent torrent:

        I cannot see the
flow, but taste it. It is
biting a coin, pure nerve-fuck

heaven! And pain is just
a feeling.

When once I danced at
traffic lights – I had been
up all night (and not alone.)

It was secret, yet I
carved our names into

        the gravel
with my heel.

Hermit

No-one sees me
fret my nervous bulk
towards the window, though
they scent my freak-indifference,
love of rock, and what it breeds:
the moss grows thicker,
doubtful, perseveres.

Last night a sparrow nested
shallow in my dream.
I woke to nothing
but the ink-cold thought
of one exclusive night, hard-edged,
and your fragility too much;
you took the table, arms ajar; your
shrunken blue-shot wrist, the iron frost.

Beat

That all-day drunk in London stink
kicks to midnight origami;
see the flower unfold to black,
the shadow who refused to budge;

a lack of certain knowledge
could not shift him; firm beneath the eye,
stage-lit; September sunlight, slanting deep,

the film of faces, rain-spat street,
raw between the teeth;
face up against it.

Limits

Knowing them, I will not care
too much; be still
be time-smacked, shocked;
all is not lost, but stops
the moment it has gone;
remains to be recovered.

Let the clocks roll on,
the evening plays
regardless; being specific to
this nest of light, this street,
this room; the window,
thinking: *is this useful?*

Ah, the coffee-fingered drag,
the dust, your ashtray kindness,
split-end rugs and incense, books.
Each morning stamps its white hum down,
essential; how to cock your wrist to stub.

Private View

First reaction: ok; clever,
kind of works but could be bigger.
How the light affects my eyes,
the colours rub against each other.
Hard to judge, though once
I felt it,
touched
the edge, was touched
directly; vertigo, electric
brush; lips on my neck,
all autumn glut, stunned
sweet September; stupid, fat with luck.

Sea Cows

Thick, late summer mist
and dapple, every evening,
creak and bellow, bulking current,
sea cows through the rusty meadow.

Where jet-bound? She looked so perfect
in that light. Don't move
a muscle; paint your house
and hope to die. She's perfect still.

Perched sideways
on the beached wreck of a thresher,
watch them come together.

PAUL STEFFAN JONES

The Age of Princes

In a house where
a famous hymn was written
he will pour the wine
so fast into my glass
it will sound like a stream
from Canaan's cracked lips.

We will look alike,
all eyebrows and height,
but are not brothers,
though cut from
the same intransigent cloth,
sewn to the suit of skin
by a wayward stitch.

We survived
the stunted emotional language
of our parents,
the calcium deficiency
of our schooling,
the deceptions
of our employment,
the impossibility
of our romances.

We will emerge from the fog
of our dispossession
and diffidence
to the torches and touchés
of our revival,
lopsidedly grinning
our good fortune,
accepting the accolades
of our revelation.

Dugger

I come to worship you
but all I get
is a fistful of fuck-all
in a country all wrapped up
in medieval packaging
and former imperial muscle wastage.

Your left hand says
you're married
but your eyes tell me
you want to be
rampant and lost
in a forest of a stranger's design.
If only I knew where to find
the key to my cage,
I would then unfold my wings
and straighten the arc
of my posture
with the thrill of the dive.

Cow and Calf

The stones know their place
claimed by the investment
in their transportation to it
and the adulation their shapes
earned and enjoyed.

Massive yet
somehow suggesting
nimbleness
and a contradictory concealment,
these are the solid sisters
who rule the moors
with their permanence
and knowledge of the skies.

In their fissures
are the remains of
winged things
that crashed there
thousands of years ago.
Beneath their lichen coats
are the fingerprints
of the old fathers
who gripped the rock
with the sure hands
of ploughmen.
In their magnet
is the power
that presaged
this dribbling age,
that calls to
the lost navigators
to return to the core.

Geranium Jones

You will be
stem and petal,
pretty,
pollen
and perennial,
leaning in a soft breeze,
as exotic as a woman,
as real as beer.

He will be
the bee,
the seed,
the summer,
blown in on
a long-exhaled breath,
what you have waited for
on your rug of roots.

New Bone

My right fist has grown a new bone
now that the imagined frontier
of manliness has been overrun
by the bandits
of political correctness
and the blood has been drained
from our living.
I develop a new pop sensibility
to complement the cheery days
and the empty crisp packets
that add colour, percussion and insult
to my street's sadness.

Pendragon

He is barbed wire torc,
polished black boots,
leather armour,
kestrel-eyed,
an acolyte of the cult of heads,
his mother's song of solstice.

He's been fighting in towns
and drowned villages
revealed in drought and dream.
Though he is a minor king
in the domain of
his making and magic,
he knows he has little time
to overthrow his oppressors
for he has studied
the assassination
of the working class
and knows by heart
the litany of the slain.

He breathes as though
he is about to burst into flames,
an endangered dragon
smouldering into the struggle
he is about to unleash,
the pack of one hundred
two-headed
cartoon hounds
he has been sketching
since his schooling.

He has the weapon
he has always coveted,
clutching it clammily
in his restless hand
in the mirror
in his grandmother's house.
He does not know
exactly how it works
but imagines
it will know what to do
when he decides to act
and all the doubters
are bowled over
by his tankist niceties.

Shiv

I live
this shiv
I give
it with
steel love
above
the tough
guy stuff
I need
to feed
the creed
I bleed
to be
just me
no fee
just free
this blade
was made
to wade
not fade
to sail
the tails
of gales
and gaols
I pledge
this edge
to etch
not judge
I am
my arm
my psalm
my harm.

Smithereen

He is held together
by a hair hatched
in the Mesopotamia
of his schoolbooks.
He feels the long lace
of his left boot work loose
as he negotiates
the surface,
unravelling as he goes.

21 Fly Salute

21 flies noiselessly occupy
my bedroom ceiling
in groups of three or four,
a different formation
each time I take a look.
Are they pestilent invaders
or aerial ballroom dancers?
Whatever their intentions,
they have brought into my home
the dryness of leaves,
the unpredictability of animals
and the golden shroud of autumn.

With The Fox

We slide through
>   the barbed wire
>   leaving behind
>   the hub-caps
>   and thrown-away condoms
>   of the other world
>   entering the cool and dark
>   of the forest
>   the undersides of leaves
our thin legs tremulous   in x-ray
>   with effort and evasion
>   and earning our lives
>   the crust of the earth
>   stiff on our whiskers
>   we don't regain
>   our breath
>   we will never regain
we have learned to merge   our breath
>   with wheat hay and hedge
>   bending like the wind
>   invisible to eyes
>   not touching the soil
>   he is my mucker
>   my brother
>   running together to
like heat or desire   insinuate the landscape
>   in order to bring
>   destruction in the fences
>   saw-teeth and moist nostril
>   patrol the bribed dark
>   gibbous moons
>   illuminate our quarry
of desolation   in the ditches
>   down on them
>   down on them
>   redcoat to
>   redcoat.

MARKUS LLOYD

I

Finches and Parakeets

"Asylum", said Dr. Meron

An aviary in the hospital grounds,
a tumult of finches and parakeets,

and, there, Elaine,
the cockatoo of her left hand held to the mesh,
its beak of sunflower seed kissing a captive full on the lips,
with tongues.

With irritable wings,
the finches and parakeets perch to *un*perch,
pinned to the spot, except where they are not.

In dressing gowns of plumage,
the birds might well be patients,
bullying for attention.

Elaine, preening, makes the most of a canary home perm
and someone else's make-up. She's allowed off ward
to see and to flirt with the finches and parakeets.

She is a girl in a Puffa Jacket,
wearing pyjamas with arrow-pierced hearts beneath,
who wants to coo over the "pretty, pretty things".

She has a thumb's-up face. Its biro'd eyes and mouth open
and the issuing laughter, spouts of water at play
on the emptiness of the afternoon.

Her body will soon dishevel the air with thoughts of flight,
of absence, and she'll call a finch or a parakeet a "cunt",

and the bird will unravel from a tic of stillness
to become a Catherine Wheel of disrupted feathering
for moment, before it's doused, made to be calm.

II
Finches and Parakeets

"Anxiety erodes" said Dr. Meron

With crayon-wings, with felt-tip song,
the finches and parakeets graffiti the aviary.
They stutter, midair, flurries of seeming thoughtfulness.
What they draw, feathering glyphs, nonsensical as calculus.

They over-elaborate the corridor between the Day Room
and side wards, to'ing and fro'ing, with going this way
and that, from biscuit tin bath to trays of seed,
to that window, where you can follow
the wind into the trees with a sway,
rocked by your heart,
back and forth.

"You should be kind to yourself" says Elaine.

The finches and parakeets saw at their plumage
on corroded stanchions, on stray wires,
against whatever there is,
to cause themselves injury.

Breadcrumbs of blood trailed to a cubicle in the
           men's toilets,
where Elaine has opened the cage door of one forearm,
yet the finches and parakeets make no escape,
they linger about, close to food and drink,
to the enclosure they know to be safe.

These finches and parakeets might well be trapeze artistes,
on their swings, with their turbulent acrobatics,
but they use wires. They hang in harness
over the shit and mould of the aviary floor.

They queue, and are always early, for meds.

III
Finches and Parakeets

"How's the libido, are you getting erections?" asked Dr. Meron

A quick peck on the cheek, no. Kiss after kiss of seed, yes.

Elaine's at the aviary. Her cuttlebone face,
bruised and grazed with makeup,
pushed into the wire mesh.
She wants to be touched,
and the bloodying rust
of the cage will do.

Elaine is a vacancy of lithium, and of valium, and of co-codamol,
and of everything prescribed, and leeched, and bled,
awaiting fulfilment. Elaine is a guesthouse, off-season.
She's the landlady on the saucy postcards, who's always up for it.
Elaine wants to fuck, to be taken somewhere, out of sight,
and made to feel immediacy, to be overwhelmed by a sense of self.

So Elaine has gel'd her yellow hair, igniting a gas ring
that fingers the pan of sky placed over it.
She has cut the sweet and sour fragrance of bed-sweats
with *eau de toilette*. And she's there,
by the aviary, in her boudoir, to seduce the birds

(in truth, the finches and parakeets are a cipher,
they embody an absence standing
with his hand, a ruffling of feathers, in hers)

"*You can have me*" says Elaine, "*I want you to have me*".

A finch with no ruff, cocks its head,
its neck a snapped matchstick,
and looks daft, and sideways at Elaine,
and tries to disentangle its song,

to unpick the knot of its thoughts
with all-fingers-and-thumbs of words,
gesturing with tics of its wings,
and saying most by flying off
through the automatic doors
back onto Nightingale ward.

"Cunt!" Elaine calls after it,
"You fucking homosexual! Fuck you, you shitty little shit!"

IV
Finches and Parakeets

"Accept the fact, you are ill" said Dr. Meron

Try never to mistake the finches and parakeets for patients.

Finches and parakeets are simple fetishes of coloured plasticine,
stuck with cocktail sticks and licks of frayed silk.
They are an occupational therapy.

"Sweethearts!" Elaine greets the aviary's inmates,
and she squeals *"aren't you pretty, little things!"*

The finches and parakeets are a choir of inane scribble,
an acrobatic troupe of scrawl. Nothing need make sense,
while they are fed, watered and enclosed.

Elaine appears to blow the aviary out like bubblegum from her lips,
as they purse and smacker kisses at the birds.
"Aren't you darling!" she tells them.

One finch has no feathers around its neck,
its head is pillared on a sinew.

Other finches are minus eyes,
with a vacant pock where the eye was pecked out.

The parakeets grind their bulbous foreheads and crests
into the metal rims of water bowls and feed trays.

"You've got to get yourself strong-minded" says Elaine.

Behind the finches and parakeets is the derelict ward
where Elaine would loiter, before her re-admittance,
where she would settle on a mattress, a nettle bed
of cans and bottles, to swap a fuck for a swig or a toke,
until she had the will and/or the means to overdose.

Better you mistake the patients for finches and parakeets.

(A minicab sounds its horn outside)

Babes, we are *not* angels, Seraphim, Cherubim or anything.
Gucci'd, Versace'd, Dolce Gabbana'd in bright raiment,
we are *well* angelic, but we're downright earthly.
We are, my sweetheart, earthy beings.
We haven't the wings, have we?
And no way do we care to unburden this world,
to vacate its paving slabs, asphalt, shag pile and parquet.
We're not about to lift ourselves up to any great height,
well, are we? Be honest, darling.
Yes, *from a great height* we are willing to fall, and daily.
Our ambitions are those of Icarus and we plummet,
graceful as fuck, sacks of potatoes, *pommes de terre*.
We are windfalls bruised by a nagging expectation
of there *having* to be more. More of what?
More of the same? Look at Adam and Eve –
having partaken of that forbidden fruit,
certain that scrumping a little knowledge would do some good,
all they learnt was *there's no return, an occurrence cannot be undone.*
Our presence, hereabouts, on Terra Firma is indelible,
a red wine stain on a satin garment,
the blood and guts of young Icarus in the dust.
Thought of us becoming angels is bloody daft,
'cos if we were anything in the pecking order of God's firmament,
we'd be "*arse*angels", dodos of epiphany.
Babes, we are human. Don't you just love it? I know you do,
resplendent in your wings of shoulder blade
and halo of champagne blonde,
eager to ensnare a club with a visitation of your Chanel No. 5.
Your flesh and dress sense are your divinity,
and definitely my saving grace.
So let's go. Heaven can wait but this minicab won't.

House Breaking

She's adept at robbing the synergism off us.
She nimbly unbuckles the mattress
and deflowers the bedclothes,
leaving us spent and me for dead.
Her succulent warmth half-inched
makes the divan, a blown egg.
She is not indelicate with her goodbye-kisses,
she takes care not to wake me, but I *am* aroused.
I think it's the sherbet of body spray,
the cucumber of newly applied makeup,
the tender-grease of her lipstick on my forehead.
Or is it the timbre of the mortise lock re-engaging
as she closes the front door behind her.
Whatever's the cause,
I will steal one off the wrist when she's gone.
Unlike her, I'm not a professional,
I haven't a getaway planned, I'm cack-handed,
and I'm wracked by guilt.
It's hard bird this unemployment.

We're no Trevor Howard and Celia Johnson,
but I could use a *Brief Encounter* in the mornings.
I'd like to run a hem down the platform
chasing her departing engine,
to linger, extant, waving,
to malinger and keep waving like a swollen windsock,
like a fist shaken, like someone who will really,
really miss her.

The Towpath

Surviving the towpath (newly resurfaced,
the asphalt dead level, unerringly pitch
black) daily. The defunct canal,
a sheet of red oxide
sealed with innumerable layers
of lacquer, is a path of cloud.
Its silver nitrate and milk of magnesia
flinches, touched by reeds
and tongue-lashes of air,
impinged on by filament-legged creatures,
eddying, buoyant. Once, a route East-West,
only barges of stratocumuli navigate
to and fro nowadays, looking for someplace
to unburden themselves.

Debtors' Holiday

With a monstrous Spanish Red, with a pocket-knife
come corkscrew, with fish and chips and cigarettes,
with greased lips and salted fingertips,
Mr & Mrs Micawber would go to the beach after hours
to be matadors. They would taunt the waves. Olé! Olé!
But the waves trampled up the sands all the same,
issuing fearsome snorts of foam and brine.
The Micawbers (not quite the Burt Lancaster
and Deborah Kerr of flotsam and jetsam)
having been up-ended and bloodied by the incoming tide
(and too pissed to make love or simply to fuck),
were quick to admit defeat. *It is the opposite direction,*
it would appear, Mrs Micawber, is the better part of valour
in these most discommodious of circumstances.
Soaked through, anaemic in the moonlight,
towelled in each other's arms, obese with caresses,
they would walk along the cliffs to their static caravan.
As they went they'd expound
on the wonder of the future they'd beget
when this Dawlish fortnight was done.
It was talk that rode the bucking bronco
of a stiff, sou'westerly breeze. Daydreams
they wished would set like concrete
and build-up into a great, impenetrable seawall.

Puff

Puff is what bolsters the wishbone and tissue
of a pigeon's strut and flight.
It's *puff* that plumps up the cushion
of a pigeon's bosom.
Puff is what makes a pigeon carry on,
tactless with its shit
and heedless of its greed.
It's the *puff* we come to loathe about pigeons.
We grow snide with shotguns,
eager to slap them down.
But it's like trying to pitchfork balloons.
Puff keeps pigeons buoyant.

For John

Don't complicate the flowers with names I have to learn,
with weeds of horticultural fact, John.
It damages the pristine sight of them.
Makes those blooms of yours mere constructs,
and not a commonplace wondrous
existing to warrant eyes.
You and your bone meal, sulphur and pinching out
get in my way, are ruinous. So, please,
don't place a sanitizing cube in the urinal of their flowering,
let them stink up the air and rampage outside of your garden
like the Japanese Knotweed of a bus station gents,
ravishing the pavement and bays.
We can just stand here, John:
the nicotine greenery of your fingers
lifting a roll-up to your gob, in awe, yeah?

Fission

In the window of a hut overripe with creosote
was the foetus of a chimpanzee
held in brackish formaldehyde,
a slumbering astronaut
stillborn in zero gravity,
preserved in a nimbus
of sallow, respiring backlight.
An incidental exhibit amid the enclosures
of the zoo. It was the only animal
ever to captivate me as a child.
Its translucent toes and fingers,
neon-fringed, were so pathetic and indelicate.
Embalmed in the bestial miasma
of meat breath, of faeces and urine,
of musk – its lack of life stank
of life. The paradox turned the world inside out.
I was cut from the womb and left to float
weightless between birth and death,
where the two collide like atoms.

KATHRYN SIMMONDS

Awake in the Far Away

I like it here: it's easier to scan the internet
for news of hurricanes
or read the rules of wrestling, or look up recipes
for Won Ton Soup.
They let me decorate the Post It notes
and stick them to reports until they're frilly
as Flamenco dancers' skirts. Olé!
There are orchids in reception.
No one writes their names on biscuit tins.

I like the boss who blushes easily and can't avoid
that luscious girl in marketing although
he tries (I've seen him pick up telephones
with no one on the other end).
I like the fug of heaters turned up full,
the clouds blown sideways
while I type *Dear Sir,*
the buses as they crawl like rainy ladybirds
down Prince of Wales Road.
And no one asks me what
I'm doing here, or if I'll stay – they simply
smile and make their way along the corridors.

There was a time before this empty board room,
I am sure, a time before this chart
flipped clean,
although it must be further off than childhood.
It's three o'clock and May;
I stand still with the tray of cups
and watch a cyclist unlock his bike.
Somewhere a telephone begins to ring.
My thoughts are turned to white stone in the sun.

Tate Modern

This is the room I return to
pacing and staring
while you are next door
watching the video
of the man
beating himself up.

Cracked roller sponge.
Abattoir light.
Cup of cold coffee,
milk skin gathered to
the star of Bethlehem.

The stepladder
is beautiful,
cordoned to keep trespassers
from climbing through the skylight,
and a shelf bears nothing
but seven silver screws
scattered like earrings.

Ladder unscalable,
screws unwearable,
cup abandoned –
oh my life!
This is the room I return to,
the room you finally tell me
is simply out of use
and not a piece of art.

Grumpy

The trees protected us from women,
as did our routine, long days of digging
followed by the scrappy evening meal,
a game of cards that I would often feel

obliged to spoil. Then she discovered us
and our poor pantomime began; the mass
of bald heads worshipping around her hips,
the wild bouquets, our jostling for the lips

that were reserved for royalty. And I could
not contain my rage against the giant God
who kept me restless with desire all night
until, half-mad, I rose and in the candlelight

I sought her mouth, a flower in the dark,
not red, but nearly black, the colour of a heart.
I kissed her and she sighed, not for my sake,
she murmured in her dream, and did not wake.

Taxi Drivers

They lean against the glossy buttocks of a cab,
kicking free of clutch and brake,

stubble-headed, right arm browner than the left,
legs whitely shocking in their shorts,

their talk, impossible to tell when distance
seals their opinions off like glass.

One lights a cigarette and blows a stream of smoke
sky-high into the station eaves.

Five cabs ahead, the leader takes a fare, shifts
into second gear, sweeps

out of the terminal and into startling sun.
Meanwhile they wait,

June sparkling on the river's filth a mile away,
the city folded tightly in their heads.

Sarah Masterson in Middle Age

"Marry the man today and change his ways tomorrow"
(Guys and Dolls)

Long before Bacardis in Havana
and the tipsy school girl act, I knew;
his suits, his casual wedge of fifty
dollar bills. His sad saint eyes.
The way he'd tip his hat at loss
then roll towards the next big win.
My sky, I free-fell into him,
and it was Paradise created
fresh in New York city every day.

Sometimes he'd disappear for three
nights at a time, then come in
early morning, glowing and unshaven.
Flush. I'd pour us coffee, scold,
then await his sure apology –
a whirl around the night-clubs
pink with dancing girls (although
he only danced with me). Until
the music faded out. Until he didn't

call home late and promise me
a rainbow wrapped in cellophane,
but started substituting *Dear* for *Doll*.
One afternoon, I found his marker
tucked inside The Book of Deutoronomy.
Listened, speechless over dinner when
he said he'd cashed his chips and what
about that little house in Maine?
Tonight he wears the crewneck

that I knitted years ago for fun.
I think of how he swung me round
and flopped me on our bed, sunlight
turning us to angels on the quilt.
I look at him, my Obadiah, paging
through *The Racing Record*, just
for old-time's sake. His dice redundant
on the shelf. My uniform dull-buttoned,
hanging in the closet out of sight.

What Not to Do with Your Day 1.

Don't make another trip to the municipal library
where you try to avoid the overweight librarian
who's spotted you one too many times already and probably
has you in a box marked 'Regular'
along with the man who trails a Tesco's carrier bag
and gabbles to the computer instructing it to
beam him up.
Don't brush your hand along the shelves, depressed
by all the works of genius you'll never read
then meander home through unconvincing sunlight
turning over the same old thoughts.
At home, don't spend three quarters of an hour at the piano
trying to master *Leaving on a Jet Plane*.
Don't return in a half hours' time for another shot.
Don't scoff three chocolate mini rolls and then feel slightly sick
or decide a cup of coffee will
'perk you up' then worry the caffeine
is staining your teeth.
Don't turn the examination of your teeth into
a search for errant facial hair
and reason that, since you're not going anywhere,
now is the time to deal with the problem.
If you have a television set, don't switch it on.
Don't watch an interview
with a star you've never heard of.
Don't bother with the kids TV show either, the one presented by
a suntanned girl who talks at you in a shouty voice.
Don't hate her for a long time afterwards for being banal
and well paid.
And as the light finally gives up, leaving you to contemplate a pile
of newspapers from last weekend,
don't decide to have a go at *Leaving on a Jet Plane*
one last time.

Afternoon Song

It is nice in the asylum – it smells of peaches all day long. Better here,
with the soft edges of the board games, than out in the rain that never
calls you by your Christian name. Here there are lights-out by eleven and
Cup-a-Soups which you can help yourself to any time you please. There
are no characters in clogs or white starch overalls – it is not that kind of
outfit – instead there is Mike who keeps a note in loopy handwriting of
'How you're getting on' and you know that if you asked to take a look,
he'd turn over the file and say 'See, nothing to hide' showing you his
palms. There are no secrets here, even during sleep; we tell each other
everything – Philip's mother chasing spoons through corridors, Meg's old
boyfriend dressed as Mary Queen of Scots. Tomorrow, we are expecting
the begonias to open, en masse, or individually, pink or orange or navy
blue: one of them, at least, is bound to blossom soon.

Against Melancholy

Pick up your mat and walk –
I speak to you who ponder
on the hoar frost turning leaves
to veiny paper hearts,

you who choose to sit
in churches, votive candles
guttering to pools of wax;
I've sat there too

a few rows back,
putting questions to the gloom,
I've seen you sobbing
for the things you miss:

resist. Don't seek out
bony trees plinked silvery with rain,
look with your other eyes,
the ones you use in dreams

to see the risen dead
walk cheerfully through corridors,
still testing doors, still curious
for new exquisite rooms.

Rodin's Lovers Interrupt their Kiss

I slid my hand from her marble thigh,
removed my tongue from her mouth
and opening my eyes found someone
leaning close enough to brush us with his lips.
Stepping down, I circled him.
My love drew back her hair
to press an ear against his heart.
We turned our heads, saw other scattered
strangers dotting space. Hand in hand
we crossed the polished floor to study them;
the grave-eyed loners, slope-armed lovers,
crocodiles of children charmed to statues
in school uniform. I touched a face in flower
beneath a canvas sun. Beyond the door
another world revolved through segments
made of glass. Traffic streaked and stopped
in front of watercolour lights which blurred
from red to green then back again.
A ribbon of brown river wound away.
Her fingers fell from mine so gently
I could hardly feel their absence afterwards.

Going to the Dogs with Mickey Rooney

Now, at eighty-something years he's shrunk to less
than five foot three, which causes some difficulty

because the crowd is dense and loud, and instead
of struggling for a view he wants to start on about

how Laurence Olivier once called him the best actor
in Hollywood, and did I know that when he first

appeared on stage he was seventeen months old,
wowing the audience by tooting a tiny mouth-organ?

He's just not getting this, I think to myself,
I haven't come to Walthamstow to hear about

Our Gang or *Babes on Broadway* – so I pass him
my binoculars, and steer him in the direction

of the bunny, a white flash streaking the track,
the lashing greyhounds in their numbered vests,

tongues lolling pink, coats glossy in the floodlight
as fresh paint. "I've got sixty quid on *Assistant*

Producer" I shout, and Mickey all at once
is clambering onto the bench, waving his arms, crying

"Move, you sonovabitch" like the Brooklyn Joe
he used to be until his mother changed his name

in 1926. Afterwards we'll get pie and peas,
discuss his wives; perhaps I'll let him play-punch me.

MICHAEL ARNOLD WILLIAMS

The Book

It was when I could not see, when I only imagined
Inclines and geometries of a locked park outside,
And lovers shackled therein, that I wrote,
In the cube of my own light.

There was too, a pain of the place,
But so much less when empty,
Populate only by spirits of the stairs,
Of men, who like me, had stared at cracks of the spiral,
As if one midnight we might all have crashed
Down through the well, mixing our times, our bones,
With stone, at the bottom of the hill.

O, o, yessy yes. I could have written a snarling chapter,
Of science, of politic, edited like silk,
Sent it to a famous broadsheet,
Or made it to a fiction's base.

Instead I wrote of history, the nature of men's memories.
I wrote in a scientific room, frosted, lonely,
To say, even after abuse, of being unable to cast off shame,
Of being still of a chapel-taught kind to not beg or lie,
Unable to fit a hand red-gloved into the beast's vagina,
I still could. I was not mad.

When I closed my eyes to destruction,
In a grime of a room denied for years a cleaner's rag,
Its tables black to touch, and encrusted, with that flake
That flies from a man's skin,
I wrote, or thought, or slept, or stared into the occult,
And leaving sands lie, wrote my pages,
Irrelevant to prospect, printed myself at that spot,
In one great palm print.

When First We Met

I remember the way her body
                    transformed garments,
The dark male shirt becoming
                    a liquid shift.

She would kneel in the moonlit room,
As restless as a birthday child,
Her braided hair an artist's brush,
                              painting my skin,

So I would writhe,
And think my whole height
                              a covered ugliness,
Too great, too raw by far.

On Noting down Inscriptions
on War Graves near Arras

With my pencil I write things written many times.
I take the lines placed here,
Read back each as if it was not one more reprise,
The Song of Solomon engraved in Arras stone,
But this man unique in his catafalque.

I take each to my page,
And by this act remember the lying of these men in all weathers;
Under sky with white cross riding cirrus over maize;
In hail on a hill of green wheat;
Through winter waters in an iron garden.

And neither do I forget the manner of their lying;
How straight, in whatever lawn.
With my pen and book I bring back these scenes,
Recall them not for honour or the document of war,
Or in iteration of the list of those sent down to sweeten Earth,
But for a knowledge of those bones themselves:

For the scapulae and hip joints, humeri and tibiae
Fibulae, radii and all the carpals of once clasping hands,
For each bone as it loosens its crystal into the artesian,
That well from which may grow the eggs of a rare bird,
The barrier reef, a child's first tooth.

Alchemy, 1941

It's night again, I see my father in his warden's coat,
Hurrying and worrying, grasping his helmet,
Looking back as he steps out where muzzles flash
                              and skies are swept white.

As the far bombs whisper at the door's latch,
I ride on the bunk's iron shawl,
In the tread of the shelter, with autumn's pale fruit.

I've seen from his shoulder: the skyline is red,
That danger's way somehow is slowed by brilliance,
Hangs like an insect in the dome.

Now how I crave to be set free, loose,
                              under sound and light,
To stare at the whole of heaven,
Wait for the precious stone to split, and ring,
And dress our village streets in steel.

Then I'd run on empty paths, searching vacant lots
To gather crystallites, imagining a happy war,

And I should be the alchemist, discoverer,
Whose chance it was to hoard the priceless ores,
Then mix and smelt, and purify rare elements
To secret sanded moulds.

The News

My father is composed entirely of words and smoke.
I arrive from a distant city, harassed, strong,
The summer highroad flickering in my eyes.

He comes to the door grasping the evening paper,
Moving at me wide-shouldered, bushy-browed,
Smoke billowing to make a stout belly.

How are you mate? he says, gripping my hand,
And I step over stone into the hallway incensed with home;
Follow him through.

He holds on to the newspaper, switches on the radio for news,
Which falls out of the gold-barred porthole of the set,
Filling the tiny back room with its weight.
Then he sits.

Mother is in a leather armchair at the other side of the grate.
I cross.
She doesn't stand, but puts up thickened arms,
Tilts her wide-featured face, and I kiss her cheek.
Isn't the news terrible she says. Quite terrible.
And she shakes her head as if she'd always expected it.

My message carries no terrors,
But the eyes of them both are filled with worries
                          they've learned from decades of struggle,
Fears from an earlier war.
Unable to notice, they sit, stationary, enwreathed,
Nursing griefs, latent cancers, afflictions of the heart.

Claustrophobia

I could even bear the circle of space:
                                        its separating drifts,
But not the box of exceptional darkness,
Soil's screening hand placed palm down,
                                        with vents closed,
As babies are murdered in their cots.

I would gladly take the left light;
                                        torch of galaxies fled,
Who's beams in angles came of fires lit
                                        before a human eye evolved,
Make it my comforter,
                                        as resting dispersed, exposed,
I made thin rime upon a planet's breath.

At the Crematorium

When everyone has left, save ourselves,
                                  a sidesman comes,
To pass the aisles clear,
To make a way for the next congregation,

But you break from me,
                            step over some low chains,
And fold yourself,
                    as only a dancer can.

Arms spread wide, forehead to the cold slate,
And I must stand, holding as still as that man
Who keeps the tapes of the horses,
                                as artillery are laid,
And orders must come to fire.

You are prostrate before a god, that only you know.
I, holding the usher away,
                          by the thin lines of my palm,
Have mourners coming to my heels,
          a fresh box borne, as battering ram for time.

I am the witness,
          as true a witness as you are true to your god.

Brussels Incident with Salt

She didn't trip, or anything like that.
                              No-one hit her.
It was in front of the crèche,
Beside the little museum,
                        on the Avenue Bertrand,
She just fainted and fell,
                        face-down in a pool of blood,
And I came by just as the other gendarme,
                              the man,
Was trying to pull her out.

We took one arm each, and lifted,
                              but her head just flopped,
And it was pouring off her chin.

A man in a small Citroen had just parked up,
                              and shot himself,
With a tiny silver six,
And this blood came like a scarlet weir
                              under the driver's door,
And you know the pavé there is rather sunken,
The people were just stepping into it,
                              spreading it about,
Treading it in Strauven's Café,
                              and the patisserie.

My wife stopped, and put her shoes into the sink,
                              with her scarf and her tights,
And a blouse.
It was a pure accident, she said,
                        poor girl,
She just fainted and fell,
                        and the blood hadn't yet congealed.
She might quite easily have drowned.
Then running the cold water tap, she added
                        several large spoons-full of table salt.

Smoke Rings, 1945

They're smoking cigars on the Devon coast,
Long steel Havannas,
Rifled of course.

And the rings rise resonant, holding their continuity,
Rolling, clinging, to make a point.

They aren't all noise these guns,
Not just a big bang,
Not simply a roar and splash, the unseen hurt.

Over the salt marsh, out from the shingle,
At Westward Ho,
The early morning party trick says:
Now, today, this very moment,
The war's won.
        The war's won.
                The bloody war's won.

And in raw celebration
Peter and I step from the slatey stones together,
Throw ourselves shouting into a cold, rough sea.

Sixty-Seven Degrees North

James draws a picture of the Arctic,
     jade sky, over the roof of the town rink,
A heated pavement,
     with birch trees confirming resilience,
Aspens like fire.

And he has: slope-backed elk,
Leggy mosquitoes waiting at windows,
       for sprung landings,
Reindeer with herd bells.

At this, the country of fathering Christmas,
     where sunrise slips under a door,
There's ourselves,
     camped out near walls of rosy stone,
By lakes, from which the tones bleed,
So all light is highlight, reflection before snow.

And we wonder for winter,
      wonder when everyone waits
On a stampede for cellars, with sour aquavit,
Count, one day more,
     one midnight of hanging aurora,
Before we're believing the bitterest breeze.

September has failed,
And James paints his portrait of young life,
     slim and wilful, and full of football,
Where under the mackerel skies,
      all trees are goalposts,
Their riffling nets tied at the ski-jumps of Lapland.

We back, pause, race for the last big kick,
      finding a corner,
The frozen stanchion,
Turn waving, sounding our engine to leave.

The Poets

Tiffany Atkinson

Tiffany Atkinson was born in Berlin in 1972 to an army family, and lived in Germany, Cyprus and various parts of Britain throughout her childhood. After studying English at Birmingham University she moved to Cardiff to take an MA and PhD in Critical Theory, and has lived in Wales ever since. She now lectures in English at the University of Wales, Aberystwyth, where she also co-hosts a weekly poetry-and-pints event. Her poetry has appeared in *Poetry Wales, New Welsh Review, Skald, New Writing 12* (Picador, 2002) and *The Pterodactyl's Wing: Welsh World Poetry* (Parthian, 2003), and she was the winner of the Cardiff International Poetry Competition in 2001. She is working on her first full-length collection of poetry.

Zoë Brigley

Born in Caerphilly in the Rhymney Valley in 1981 Zoë Brigley had much encouragement from the Welsh Academi as a child and subsequently completed a BA in English Literature and Creative Writing at the University of Warwick with first class honours. Widely published, she is also an experienced performer of her poetry. She won an Eric Gregory Award in 2003 and received an Academi bursary in 2005. She currently divides her time between completing a PhD on contemporary Welsh women poets, and freelance writing and editing for various magazines and journals. With her mother, Jude Brigley, a performance poet and dedicated teacher, she will be co-editing an anthology of Welsh women poets for Honno press. She also works part time as the Welsh Editor for the Heaventree Press, based in Coventry.

Abi Curtis

Abi Curtis was born in Rochford, England in 1979 and lives in Brighton. She has a BA in Literature/Cultural and Community studies from the University of Sussex, and an MA in Creative Writing from the University of Exeter. She is currently back at the University of Sussex, working on a DPhil in Creative and Critical Writing, which combines her love of writing with her interest in psychoanalysis. An enthusiastic reader, a writer of fiction as well as poetry, she has been published in a number of small magazines and anthologies and is working on her first full-length collection of poetry. An early draft received an Eric Gregory Award in 2004.

Karen Goodwin

Born in Swansea in 1976, Karen Goodwin has a degree in English Literature from Aberystwyth University and a Masters in Creative Writing from the University of East Anglia. Her poems have appeared in a number of literary magazines and she received an Eric Gregory Award in 2000 from the Society of Authors. She currently lives in Nicosia, Cyprus, where she works as a Community Liaison Officer. The history and landscape of Cyprus have helped inspire her recent poems. She is currently working on her first full-length collection.

Viki Holmes

Viki Holmes was born in St. Austell, Cornwall in 1975 and came to Cardiff in 1998 to work and study English literature and the Welsh language. Her first appearance in the Welsh poetry scene was as a member of the Happy Demon poetry collective in 2000. Her poetry has appeared in magazines and anthologies internationally, and her dramatic monologues have been performed by the Riuth Is Stranger Than Richard Theatre Company in Cardiff. She was a finalist in the John Tripp Award for Spoken Poetry in 2003 and 04 and has published poems in Wales, England, Tasmania, and most recently, Hong Kong, where she is working as an English teacher in a Buddhist kindergarten. She is currently working on a collection which explores the relationship between music and memory.

Rhiannon Hooson

Rhiannon Hooson was born in 1980 in Knighton, Powys, in the Welsh borders, and spent her childhood in rural Mid-Wales until moving to the North West six years ago. She has a Master's Degree (with Distinction) in Creative Writing from Lancaster University. She has published poems in a number of journals and has had a collection shortlisted for the Eric Gregory Award. She has a pamphlet out called *This Reckless Beauty* and is currently working on her first novel titled *The Midnight Tyrant*. Her plans include a PhD which will explore the notion of 'simultaneous texts' and take its inspiration from classical mythology and structuralist theory. Her research interests include the notion of female aggression and the figure of the warrior within epic and heroic poetry.

Huw Jones
Huw Jones was born in Birmingham in 1973 to Welsh parents. Brought up in the West midlands, he spent a lot of time in Wales as he was growing up. After a degree in History from Manchester University, he moved to Cambridge, where he is currently Assistant Librarian at Gonville & Caius College. He has just recently begun to have his poetry published in literary magazines. He has been involved in workshops at local schools, and given occasional readings of his work.

Paul Steffan Jones
Born in Cardigan in 1961, Paul Steffan Jones began his career writing in the context of the Welsh language rock music world. This included performing on the radio, writing lyrics for groups and being featured in an anthology published by Y Lolfa called *Y Tren Olaf Adref*. His recent English language poems have been published widely in magazines. He works as a civil servant "currently involved in industrial action to protect vital jobs and services to the most vulnerable people in an increasingly marginalized homeland". The writers he most admires include: Dylan Thomas, Charles Bukowski, Osip Mandelshtam, Franz Kafka, Peter Matthiessen and George Orwell. He derives much inspiration from the landscapes of Wales, and numbers among his other interests: warfare, forensic science and Amerindian history.

Markus Lloyd
Born in Barry, South Wales in 1966, Markus Lloyd was educated at Pencoed Comprehensive and studied Painting at Howard Gardens, Cardiff and WSCAD, Farnham, Surrey, where he received a BA (Hons). He has lived in Llanharan, Salisbury and Southampton and has had a number of jobs including assistant gamekeeper, agricultural labourer and insurance clerk. He has published a number of poems in magazines and has also co-published a few artist books: *HOLD* with printer Tanya Rutland, (limited edition), *FatWetBed*, pamphlet. envelopes no. 1, 2, 3, 4 (limited editions). He has recently completed an MPhil in Creative Writing at the University of Glamorgan.

Kathryn Simmonds

Was born in Hertfordshire in 1972. She was educated at Loreto College in St. Albans and studied Publishing and English at Oxford Brookes University before going on to work in book publishing. In 1999 she quit her job to travel, and on returning to England took an MA in Creative Writing at the University of East Anglia. Among her favourite writers are Frank O'Hara, Bob Dylan and Flannery O'Connor. She received an Eric Gregory Award in 2002 and has published poems in a number of magazines. Her short stories have appeared in print and been broadcast on Radio 4. She has done a variety of jobs, few of them glamorous, and is now happily employed as a quiz writer and editor. Her pamphlet 'Snug' was a winner in the Poetry Business competition in 2003 and is published by Smith/Doorstop Books. She lives in north London and is working on a radio play.

Michael Arnold Williams

Born in Newport, Monmouthshire in 1936, Michael Williams was brought up at Caerleon. He read Botany at King's College, London University, and did military service as a communications engineer in the Royal Corps of Signals. He re-trained at University College, London, and worked as a Biochemist at Hammersmith Hospital, where he did a PhD on Kidney Transplantation. Subsequently, he was Lecturer and later Professor, in the Anatomy Department at Sheffield University, and did a great deal of research on locating chemical processes within cells, a subject on which he wrote two books. In the course of his research he travelled widely, lecturing and teaching in other countries including The Netherlands, France, Norway, Sweden, Romania, Yugoslavia, New Zealand, the USA and Canada. A shift in his output from Science towards the Creative Arts began in the early 1990's, and he completed the MA in Creative Writing (with Distinction) from Leeds University in 2000.

Acknowledgements

Thanks are due to the editors of the following publications where some of these poems first appeared:

Tiffany Atkinson: 'Woman Running', 'Persistent Cough' and 'Aberystwyth Short Fiction' have been published in SKALD. 'For a Housewarming' was in *New Welsh Review*. 'The Anatomy Lesson' was in *The Pterodactyl's Wing: Welsh World Poetry* (Parthian, 2003).

Zoë Brigley: 'XIX. She' and 'XXI. Trade' were both in *Poetry Wales*. 'My Dress Hangs Here' and 'Space-Time' appeared in *New Welsh Review*. 'The Clarinet Player' was in *Reactions 4*, 'X. My Grandfather' was in *Limelight*. 'XIII. A Small Unit of Time' was published in *Stride*.

Abi Curtis: 'The Cupboard' won 2nd prize in the Essex Poetry Competition in 2004.

Viki Holmes: 'postcard no. 1' appeared in *New Welsh Review* and was anthologised in *The Big Book of Cardiff* (Seren, 2005).

Rhiannon Hooson: 'Crugybyddar' first appeared in *Borderlines*. 'Tracking' was in *Rain Dog*. 'Wintering' was published in *Mslexia*. 'Storm Gazing at Orrest Head' was in *Coffee House*. 'The Sin Eater' was in *Poetry Wales*.

Huw Jones: 'Progress' appeared in *Stride*. 'Limits' was in *Poetry Wales*.

Paul Steffan Jones: 'Shiv' was published in the anthology *The Slab of Faith* (Muesli Jellyfish).

Markus Lloyd: ' Puff' has appeared in *New Welsh Review*.

Kathryn Simmonds: 'Afternoon Song', 'What Not to Do with Your Day 1' and 'Going to the Dogs with Mickey Rooney' all appeared in *Exquisite Corpse*. 'Grumpy' was featured on *boomeranguk.com*. 'Rodin's Lovers Interrupt their Kiss' was in the UEA's *New Writing* Anthology 2004.

Michael Arnold Williams: 'The Book' and 'Sixty-Seven Degrees North' appeared in *Poetry London*. 'When First We Met', 'On Noting Down Inscriptions on War Graves near Arras', 'Alchemy, 1941', 'The News', and 'Claustrophobia' were in *Poetry Wales*. 'Brussels Incident with Salt' was in *Smiths Knoll*.